JEREMIAH

UNUSUAL SERMONS

Dr. Mike Smith

Franklin Publishing

PRINCETON, TEXAS

Kelly Carr / Franklin Publishing
1215 Juniper
Princeton, Texas 75407

www.FranklinPublishing.org

Ordering Information:

Quantity sales. Special discounts are available on quantity purchases by corporations, associations, and others. For details, contact the "Special Sales Department" at the address above.

Except where otherwise indicated, all Scripture quotations are taken from the New King James Version®. Copyright © 1982 by Thomas Nelson. Used by permission. All rights reserved.

Jeremiah: Unusual Sermons / Mike Smith. —1st ed.

ISBN-13: 978-1-952064-01-2
ISBN-10: 1-952064-01-5

Contents

Dedication

I picture Jeremiah as a rugged, fearless man, yet with a tender heart that weeps for his people. Vance Zinn was a giant of a man. Literally 6 feet 5 inches and 500 pounds. Earlier in his life, he had a tumor that caused growth. He was bold in his preaching, yet he would cry nearly every sermon. He was a mentor. He was a friend. We ate a lot together. The pizza buffets would ask us to leave after an hour. We prayed together. We had a lot of theological discussions. I thank God for bringing Vance Zinn into my life. So, I dedicate this book on Jeremiah to him. I miss you, Brother Zinn.

1 The word which came to Jeremiah from the LORD, saying,
2 Arise, and go down to the potter's house, and there I will cause thee to hear my words.
3 Then I went down to the potter's house, and, behold, he wrought a work on the wheels.
4 And the vessel that he made of clay was marred in the hand of the potter: so he made it again another vessel, as seemed good to the potter to make it.

–Jeremiah 18:1-4 (KJV)

Introduction to Jeremiah

JEREMIAH 1:1-3

Any serious Bible study should first begin with a review of the 5 W's. The 5 W's are:

- Who?
- What?
- When?
- Where?
- Why?

So, before we expound upon the text, let's review these basic questions concerning Jeremiah.

WHO?

WHO WROTE JEREMIAH?

JEREMIAH

Jeremiah 1:1, "The words of Jeremiah..." For years there was no objection to Jeremiah being the author until German higher criticism, when Wellhausen placed some doubt.

Now Jeremiah 36:4 records, "Then Jeremiah called Baruch the son of Neriah: and Baruch wrote from the mouth of Jeremiah all the words of the LORD..."

Jeremiah received the words from God and dictated them to his secretary Baruch who wrote them down.

Who was Jeremiah?

Jeremiah 1:1-2 tell us three things. Jeremiah was:

Child of Hilkiah. Hilkiah was a priest. This means Jeremiah was a PK, a preacher's kid. He grew up in a religious home. I have a special place in my heart for Preacher kids. If they come to Jacksonville College I usually give them a Presidential scholarship. I have two Pk"s of my own and they are special to me.

City of Anathoth. Anathoth was a small village three miles north of Jerusalem.

Call of God. "The word of the LORD came..." to him. We will look at the call in-depth later.

WHAT?

WHAT IS JEREMIAH?

MAJOR PROPHET

Remember your Bible divisions and the type of literature in each division.

1. Law – 5 Books
    a. Genesis
    b. Exodus
    c. Leviticus
    d. Numbers
    e. Deuteronomy
2. History – 12 Books
    a. Joshua

b. Judges

c. Ruth

d. 1 & 2 Samuel

e. 1 & 2 Kings

f. 1 & 2 Chronicles

g. Ezra

h. Nehemiah

i. Esther

3. Wisdom/Poetry – 5 Books

a. Job

b. Psalms

c. Proverbs

d. Ecclesiastes

e. Song of Solomon

4. Major Prophets – 5 Books

a. Isaiah

b. Jeremiah

c. Lamentations

d. Ezekiel

e. Daniel

5. Minor Prophets – 12 Books

a. Hosea

b. Joel

c. Amos

d. Obadiah

e. Jonah

f. Micah

g. Nahum

h. Habakkuk

i. Zephaniah

j. Haggai

k. Zechariah

l. Malachi

What is the difference in major prophets and minor prophets? The size of the book, not the content or message.

WHEN?

WHEN WAS JEREMIAH WRITTEN?

600 B.C.

Jeremiah covers a period of about 56 years from 642-586 B.C. Jeremiah lived under 7 kings.

1. Manasseh – 697-642 B.C.
   a. 2 Kings 21:1-6, "Manasseh was 12 years old when he began to reign, and he reigned fifty and five years in Jerusalem.... And he did that which was evil in the sight of the LORD.... For he built up again the high places which Hezekiah his father had destroyed; and he reared up altars for Baal.... And he made his son pass through fire...."
   b. Manasseh was king when Jeremiah was born.
   c. Manasseh was Hezekiah's son. Hezekiah was a good King. Manasseh was an evil king. probably the worst in Judah's history. He built altars to pagan gods. He sacrificed his own son.
2. Amon – 642-640 B.C.
   a. 2 Chronicles 33:21-25, "Amon was two and twenty years old when he began to reign, and he reigned two years in Jerusalem. But he did evil in the sight of the LORD, as did Manasseh his father.... And his servants conspired against him, and slew him...."
   b. Amon was Manasseh's son and he followed him in his evil ways. His own servants killed him.

3. Josiah – 639-608 B.C.

    a. 2 Chronicles 34:1, "Josiah was eight years old when he began to reign, and he reigned in Jerusalem one and thirty years. And he did that which was right in the sight of the LORD...."

    b. Josiah was a good king. He honored God. He restored the Temple as a place to worship God. God allowed a priest, probably Jeremiah's father, to find the book of Deuteronomy (2 Chronicles 34:15). This is why you can see much of Deuteronomy in Jeremiah. Josiah died in a battle at Carchemish in 608 (2 Chronicles 35).

4. Jehoahaz – 608 B.C.

    a. 2 Chronicles 36:1-3, "Then the people of the land took Jehoahaz the son of Josiah and made him king....He reigned three months."

    b. Jehoahaz reigned three months then Egypt removed him and replaced him with another of Josiah's sons.

5. Jehoiakim – 608-597 B.C.

    a. 2 Chronicles 36:4, "And the king of Egypt made Eliakim his brother king over Judah and Jerusalem and turned his name to Jehoiakim. And Necho took Jehoahaz his brother and carried him to Egypt."

    b. Jehoiakim was an evil king. He turned the people back to idolatry. He made life hard for Jeremiah. God allowed Babylon's King Nebuchadnezzar to take him away.

6. Jehoiachin – 597 B.C.

    a. 2 Chronicles 36:9, "Jehoiachin was eight years old when he began to reign, and he reigned three months and ten days in Jerusalem and he did that which was evil in the sight of the LORD."

b. King Nebuchadnezzar took Jehoiachin away to Babylon and placed Zedekiah as king.

7. Zedekiah 597-586 B.C.

   a. 2 Chronicles 36:11, "Zedekiah was one and twenty years old when he began to reign and reigned eleven years in Jerusalem."

   b. Zedekiah was the third son of Josiah to reign over Judah. He was weak and compromising.

   c. Nebuchadnezzar, King of Babylon, invaded Jerusalem three times, in 605, 597, and 586. In 586 he destroyed the Temple.

   d. 2 Chronicles 36:13 says, "...he stiffened his neck and hardened his heart from turning unto the LORD God of Israel."

   e. Nebuchadnezzar appointed Gedaliah as governor over Jerusalem. Jeremiah fled to Egypt.

WHERE?

WHERE WAS JEREMIAH WHEN HE WROTE THE BOOK?

JERUSALEM

Most of Jeremiah's life was spent around Jerusalem, the chief city of the Southern Kingdom, Judah.

When Jeremiah was preaching, the three main world powers were:

1. Assyria to the north

   a. In 722b.c. Israel, the northern Kingdom, fell to Assyria.

2. Egypt to the South

3. Babylon to the East

WHY?

WHY WAS JEREMIAH WRITTEN?

JUDGEMENT AND HOPE

Book could be outlined:
Introduction: Who, What, When, Where and Why
1. Call – Jeremiah 1
2. Creative Sermons – Jeremiah 2-24
3. Conflict – Jeremiah 25-29
4. Covenant – Jeremiah 30-33
5. Collapse – Jeremiah 34-39
6. Countries – Jeremiah 40-45
7. Conclusion – Jeremiah 46-52

1

Jeremiah's Call
Jeremiah 1:4-19

INTRODUCTION

As we work our way through the text, some observations must be shared.

1. God creates – 1:5

- We know Jeremiah had biological parents. Jeremiah 1:1 says he was the son of Hilkiah. But Jeremiah 1:5 strongly reminds us that God is the one who creates us. Physical birth is not our beginning. Yes, life begins at conception, but in reality, it begins in the mind of God. Verse 5 says "Before I formed you in the belly, I knew you."

- Pro-abortion people say life does not begin until birth. The Bible is clear that life begins at conception. A fetus is a person. To abort is wrong.

- This verse should give comfort to all mothers who experienced miscarriages. God knew your baby. Even to those who live with the guilt of abortion, God knows your baby. See, God is creator. That's why as Christians we must pray for making abortion illegal.

2. God calls.

   a. Read Jeremiah 1:5. "Before thou came forth out of the womb I sanctified thee, and I ordained thee a prophet unto the nations." Jeremiah was born into a priest's home, yet God calls him to be a prophet.

A priest represented the people to God.

A prophet represented God to the people.

A priest was more traditional.

A prophet was more untraditional.

A priest usually had a simple, routine life.

A prophet had an unusual, unpredictable life.

A priest performed ceremonies.

A prophet preached conviction.

A priest comforted the people.

A prophet confronted the people.

A priest dealt with outward symbols.

A prophet dealt with hearts and sin.

b. Jeremiah's call was to be a prophet. Let's look at this call.

- There is a general call to all for salvation.

  ▪ I believe the gospel is to be clearly proclaimed unto all the nations. From man's point of view, we should seek to clearly share Jesus with all.

  ▪ From God's point of view, He knows who will be saved for salvation is of God.

- There is a specific call to service.

  ▪ Every Christian is given gifts for service.

  ▪ Jeremiah's specific call was to be a prophet unto the nations.

  ▪ I remember very plainly my general call to salvation and my specific call to service.

SALVATION

I grew up in a home with parents who took me to church. I knew the Bible stories, but it was not personal until 11 years of age. At the end of a sermon while the invitation was extended, God convicted me of my sin and lostness. I asked my friend Joey if he wanted to go down and he said he already had, so I went down and told Brother Alvin Bell I wanted to be saved. That was my general call.

SERVICE

My specific call was first met with resistance, like Jeremiah's. Verse 1:6 says, "God, I cannot speak, I am a child."

I tried to argue with God that I am shy and timid. I tried to convince Him to let me make a lot of money to give to Him. The night before I was to sign a letter of intent to play football at Texas A&M, my dad came into my room and said, "Mike, tomorrow you have to tell them yes or no." He left, and I got on my knees beside my bed and prayed. God's presence was real and sometime during the night I surrendered to God's specific call to serve Him. I later made it public before the church. I like to tell my Aggie friends I am really not sure if God called me to preach that night or just saved me from becoming a Texas Aggie.

GOD'S COMMISSION TO JEREMIAH

Jeremiah 1:10, "See, I have this day set thee over the nations and over the kingdoms, to root out, and to pull down, and to destroy, and to throw down, to build, and to plant."

Look at Verse 11.

- I see a rod of an almond tree
- This was a sign that spring was near. What tree in your area lets you know spring is near. Jeremiah was sent and commissioned to tell the people that the judgment of God was near.

Look at Verse 13

- I see a seething pot. A seething pot is one that is about to boil over. Jeremiah had the assignment to tell the people that God had enough and His judgment was about to come down on them.

Look at verse 18

- I have made thee an iron pillar
- God always followed his message with hope. The iron pillar was a reminder that while judgement was coming He was an iron pillar and no harm come to His people that He did not allow.

Look at verse 10

Jeremiah's message was intended to ...

- Root out---he was to dig deep into the core sin of the people and expose it
- Pull down—he was to destroy the false idols in the land
- Throw down----Man had lifted up false gods. Jeremiah was to throw them down
- Build and plant---Jeremiah was to rebuild truth and worship of one true God.

Jeremiah was not a popular preacher and the people did not like his message. He was an upstream voice of God in a downstream world. Jeremiah had a tough assignment.

What assignment has God given you?

2

Jeremiah's Creative Sermons
Jeremiah 2-24

INTRODUCTION

When I first started preaching, children's sermons were becoming very popular. Very few churches have them today.

This was a time all children would come to the front of the sanctuary and the pastor would usually have an object and preach a sermon holding that object.

Example:

- The Pastor holds a key and talks about how Jesus is the key to our success.
- The Pastor holds up a dirty glass of water and says that this is a life of sin. Then he pours red solution in and the water becomes clear. He talks about the blood of Jesus.

- When I entered seminary I took a childhood education course. The teacher ask how many of us preachers did children sermons. I proudly raised my hand. She shouted back, "Stop it." She said children cannot think abstract but only concrete. She said they do not understand your children's sermons. I do not know if they did or not but they got a piece of candy and a special time with the pastor. Most of the congregation would comment, "We got a lot out of your children's sermon today."
- I received more comments on the children's sermon than my regular sermon.
- Jeremiah is full of object lessons. God would have Jeremiah go and watch or go and do strange things to try to get Judah to repent.

In this section, we will review in summary form these sermons. The main theme is repentance.

Turn from their sin and turn back to God.

DIVORCE - JEREMIAH 2-4

One preacher called this section "God files for divorce."

Look at 2:9, "Wherefore I will yet plead with you..."

Look at 3:1, "They say, if a man put away his wife..."

This scene describes a divorce. How does divorce happen? The problem is:

1. The Honeymoon is over.

Listen to 2:2, "...Thus saith the LORD; I remember thee, the kindness of thy youth, the love of thine espousals..."

    a. Several places in scripture Israel is pictured as a loving wife.

- God had passion for his people (v. 3).
- God provided for His people (v.7).

b. Yet we see: They turned from God.

Verse 2:13, "...they have forsaken me the fountain of living waters, and hewed them out cisterns, broken cisterns, that can hold no water."

2. Plea to return.

    a. Usually in a marriage when one is unfaithful, they plead with the other to work it out.

    b. Jeremiah uses 4 pictures to describe the nation of Judah:

- Unfaithful wife – 3:1-10
- Unhealthy backsliding pattern – 3:21-25
- Unplowed field – 4:1-3
- Uncircumcised heart – 4:4

    c. Usually in a divorce, one partner is unfaithful.

3. Promise to divorce – 3:6

God warns Judah. Look, I divorced Israel (v.8) and I will divorce you.

4. Pain of divorce – 4:19-31

    a. Jeremiah is known as the weeping prophet.

    b. In divorce, when all the anger is released, a lot of crying occurs.

- 1 out of every 2 marriages ends in divorce.
- I see the problem of divorce in college students.

    c. We all see pain.

- You experience pain.
- I contend even more pain

    d. Number of people who are unfaithful to God

- 15 Million Baptist
- 5 Million Best Sunday attend church
- 1 Million 20% give and do 80% of what is done in church

Along with the divorce message is the term backsliding. Jeremiah 3:8, 11, 12, 14. Hosea used term backsliding heifer. I know about backsliding heifers. God calling His people back from drifting away from Him. I grew up in Houston Texas with neighbors all around and concrete streets. One end of the street was a convenient store we called china man store because a man from China owned it. I could get a nickel coke there. The other end was a strip mall with a movie theater and a drug store with a soda fountain that made delicious malts.

Saturday routine was to sleep late, go to the movies and then get a chocolate malt. I had it made. What a good life.

Then one day my dad came home and without a discussion or family vote he declared that we were moving to Raccoon Bend Texas. I said, "Where?" This was a deserted wilderness on the Brazos River bottom in an oilfield camp. My dad thought I needed country life. He bought pigs for me to feed every day before I went to school and every evening when I returned from school. He bought baby calves that required me to mix their milk and feed in buckets. They would knock me down at least once every day.

I thought, what I did I do to make my dad so mad to move me to such a life.

He entered me into the Austin County Fair calf scrabble. There were 50 boys on one end of the arena and 25 calves on the other end of the area. They handed us a halter, which I had never seen before and said when they fired the gun for us to go get a calf and put the halter on it and bring across the finish line and the calf would be ours to keep. When the gun was fired all the boys ran to the end of the arena where the calves were. They scattered. I was built then as I still am today. I was not made for running. So I walked a few feet away from the finish line and there came a white faced calf. I grabbed her. Not knowing how to put the halter on her I just put it around her neck and started pulling her. The rope choked her and she would not move. The more I pulled and the tighter the rope around her neck got she started sliding backwards and just sat down. I thought I heard her sing, "I shall not be moved". The harder I pulled the more she would go backwards. Someone said grab her tail. I reached back and pulled her tail. She jumped up and she pulled me across the finish line. That was my first experience with a backsliding heifer.

Now I have worked with Baptist churches for fifty years and have dealt with a lot of backsliding heifers. In this analogy of divorce, God was trying to get Jeremiah to see how His people had slid away from Him and were unfaithful to Him.

DON'T COME TO CHURCH - JEREMIAH 7

Jeremiah 7 is a picture of God telling Jeremiah to go to the door of the Temple and tell the people to repent.

This seems strange. People are coming to a good place, the Temple. They come to a place of worship. Yet God tells the preacher to tell them to repent.

I mean, you expect God to tell the preacher to go to the beer joint, go to the abortion clinic, go to where they sell lottery tickets, go to the house of prostitution. Yet, God tells him to go to the church.

Why? Because they were not listening to or obeying God's word.

It is dangerous to come to church week after week and yet not heed the word of God. Too many people are caught up in religious activity and don't hear God's word.

God warns them in V. 15-16, "I will cast you out of my sight...I will not hear thee..."

I wonder how people would react if their pastor this Sunday stood at the door of the church and as people tried to enter he said repent. You can't enter until you repent.

DISGUSTING GIRDLE - JEREMIAH 13:1-10

God tells Jeremiah to put on a girdle. In our culture, we think of that as woman's wear. In Jeremiah's day, it was part of the priestly clothing. It was a symbol of service.

He tells Jeremiah, don't wash it. How disgusting to wear a dirty, smelly piece of clothing.

But it gets worse.

God tells Jeremiah to go to the River Euphrates that is 400 miles away. It is a 3-month walk. He obeys and when he arrives, God tells him to bury the girdle. He does. Then he walks 3 months back. Then God tells him to go back, and that is 3 months there and 3 months back. He is to dig up the old, rotten girdle and bring it back to Jerusalem. He does. A year of walking. Then he has to wear the disgusting girdle. It was rotten, smelly.

The message is this: Your service stinks to me.

This should be a wake-up call for all of us.

What does God think of our service?

DROUGHT - JEREMIAH 14

I lived in West Texas for 7 years. The area was noted for its dry land cotton farming. By this, I mean farmers were totally dependent on God sending rain. There was no irrigation. Up on the caprock around Lubbock, farmers there irrigated their crops. Dry land farming is tough. I often heard farmers say if they make a crop every five years, they could make it.

In Jeremiah's day, they were totally dependent on God for rain. Not only for crops, but also for drinking water.

God would send a drought to get the people's attention. When the people got into trouble, they turned to God and prayed.

Does God cause every storm or catastrophe? Well, some things are in motion, like seasons and weather patterns. God is certainly aware. It is a fact that after every problem – 9-11, storms, etc., we see an increase in church attendance, then it dwindles back down. It may seem cruel but God often will use crisis, storms, and problems to get our attention. Your relationship with Him is more important than your happiness, comfort or health.

DON'T MARRY - JEREMIAH 16

Jewish men were expected to marry by the age of twenty. In fact, rabbis pronounced a curse on any who refused to marry and begat children.

Jeremiah was told not to marry.

I am sure a wife could have been an encouragement to him.

But he was not to marry as a symbolic act to show Judah that families will die by the sword, starve to death, or be taken captive by Babylon. Every time someone asked Jeremiah why he didn't marry, he could respond – the coming of God's judgement.

DIVINE POTTER'S HOUSE - JEREMIAH 18

Jeremiah was told to go to the potter's house and watch.

I lived in Edom, Texas, for 3 years. Edom is an arts and crafts town. They had a knifemaker, silversmith, jewelry maker, glass blower, and Potter Brown.

I would often go and watch Potter Brown make pottery. He shipped it all over the world.

As Jeremiah watched the potter, he learned some valuable lessons.

1. The Divine Potter has power over human clay.

The potter can shape and make whatever he wishes with clay. The clay does not know what it will look like or be. But the potter knows.

God has a plan for our life. We don't always know or understand that plan. That is why we should seek God, not resist him.

2. The Divine Potter threw away marred pieces.

As the potter was working with clay, he encountered a marred, hard piece. He could not make his object until he took out the marred piece.

It's like God is working in our life. If we allow sin to harden our heart, we will resist God. God's plan can be delayed if we allow sin to remain.

We must repent of sin.

3. The Divine Potter then reshapes the clay.

God is a God of second chances.

DEATH TO TRADITIONS - JEREMIAH 35

Traditions are good but can be a hinderance to growth.

Rechabites were nomadic people who did not drink wine. This was their tradition.

God told Jeremiah to go set a bottle of wine in front of them. This seems strange that God would tell a preacher to buy wine and tempt people.

The lesson here was to show the people of Judah that Rechabites were more faithful to their traditions than they were to God.

This reminds us not to live by tradition but by the word of God.

God gave Jeremiah a tough assignment.

I wonder how Jeremiah would be received today.

By and large, people today don't like hard preaching against sin.

Today, people pick a church by their music, or children's programs, or by their amenities. By that, I mean, do they provide a coffee shop, a workout room, and a handball court? I am not saying those things are sinful. But I am saying you should pick a church where the word of God is being preached. Chapter 6:16 says, "...ask for the old paths..."

I am not one who wants to go backwards. I am thankful for air conditioning, heat, comfortable pews, inside plumbing, and a baptistry. My first church King had no water. The restroom was an outhouse. We baptized in Cow House Creek. I'm thankful today that the old path is preaching of God's word.

3

Conflict
Jeremiah 19-29

DEALING WITH CONFLICT

Conflict is real. Everyone experiences conflict in one form or another. I attend a lot of 50th wedding anniversary celebrations. Sometimes you hear a speech from the couple, and they say, "We've been married 50 years and never had a cross word." Liar, liar, pants on fire." No one can have a relationship for 50 years and not have conflict.

Jeremiah experienced conflict his whole ministry. He had conflict with religious and political leaders. When your message is judgement, doom and gloom, you are not going to be asked back as a preacher. Let's see what we can learn from Jeremiah's conflict.

Let's see what we can learn from Jeremiah's conflict.

CONFLICT WITHIN

Look at Jeremiah 19:14-15. Jeremiah goes to the steps of the church and preaches evil and destruction. Look at Jeremiah 20:1-2. The priest and governor, Pashur, physically beats Jeremiah and throws him in jail. Jeremiah experiences real physical pain. The stocks are in a public area for all to see, so it also brings shame with the pain.

DOUBTS HIS CALL - JEREMIAH 20:7-18

In verses 7-8, Jeremiah doubts his call. He feels God has deceived him. The word here for deceived carries a picture of being seduced. Jeremiah feels like God tricked him into ministry. But in truth, God has been up-front with him.

Verses 9-10, Jeremiah thinks about quitting. He decides to keep his mouth shut. He thinks "I just won't preach." But that didn't work, for the message was burning in him.

Jeremiah didn't preach because he had to say something. No, he had something to say.

DEPRESSION - JEREMIAH 20:14-18

He curses the day he was born." Why didn't God just kill me in the womb? No, he had to let me be born and live a life of shame."

What to do with pain.

1. Pray--------Take it to the Lord. Verse 10.

God can handle our doubts. Pashur's name changes to Magor-missabib, which means terror on every side. People in the Bible often suffered hardships.

Job – His wife tried get him curse God and die.

Elijah – Under a tree - 1 Kings 19:4

David in a cave – Psalm 57

Jonah in a fish – Jonah 2

Jesus on a cross – Mark 27:46

2. *Praise God in the midst of suffering. Verse 11.*

3. *Push on through.*

Remember:

- Jeremiah 1:5
- Ephesians 1:4

CONFLICT AROUND YOU SEEN AS DERELICTION OF DUTY - JEREMIAH 23:1-8

Jeremiah has a strong word to the preachers. Instead of leading they were driving, they didn't care or minister to the people. Jeremiah chapter 23 is one of the most condemning chapters toward pastors of any in Gods word.

DISGRACEFUL CONDUCT - JEREMIAH 23:9-15

What the false prophets were doing made Jeremiah sick. False prophets had led the Northern Kingdom of Israel astray. Now false prophets were leading the Southern Kingdom astray. Whenever a nation needs healing, it is usually because God's people are not obeying. We like to blame dishonest politicians. We like to blame immoral people. God blames the preachers.

2 Chronicles 7:14

DISHONEST MESSAGE - JEREMIAH 23:16-32

False prophets offer false hope. Verse 16.

Their words are not from God. False prophets say things like "Send me $5.00 so you can be blessed" or "Give me seed money so you can be rich."

DECEITFUL CALL - JEREMIAH 23:21

God did not call them.

They had no burden of the people.

Today some churches' emphasis is on fun and entertainment instead of the burden of crying.

Illustration - Jeremiah 24

This is the story of good figs and bad figs. Bad figs were those who disobeyed God.

These were those who stayed in Jerusalem. They thought they were favorite sons. They thought they would be blessed. God had told them to go. But they didn't want to go for they knew it would mean suffering.

CONFLICT WITHOUT - JEREMIAH 25

Four times in this message Jeremiah preaches judgement.

Here he tells them the Babylonian captivity will last 70 years.

The law of Sabbath is ignored for 500 years. See 2 Chronicles 36:20-21 and Leviticus 25:3-5.

The Judgement of the nation 15-30

He used picture illustrations:

- Cup of wrath – vs 15-24
- Roaring lion; fear – vs. 30 & 31
- Winepress – Joy – but God does shout – vs. 30b
- Lawsuit – vs. 31

- Storm – vs. 32-33
- Refuse – garbage – vs. 33
- Broken pottery – vs. 34
- Slaughtered flock – vs. 34-35

Illustration - Jeremiah 27

- Yoke – sign of submission; they would not submit so God puts a yoke on them – v. 7

4

Covenant
Jeremiah 30-33

In the Bible there are 7 covenants. The word covenant means agreement. A covenant is a contract. In the case of the Bible, covenants are agreements or contracts between God and man.

These seven covenants will either be between God and man in general or God and Israel.

These seven covenants will either be conditional or unconditional.

A conditional covenant is when God says if you do this, then I will do this.

An unconditional covenant is when God says I am going to this regardless of what you do.

Let's review briefly these seven covenants.

1. Adamic covenant

    Genesis 3:15-19
    Man, in general
    Unconditional

It is curses pronounced against mankind for the sin of Adam and Eve.

2. Noahic covenant

> Genesis 9
> Man, in general
> Unconditional

Promise not to destroy the earth by flood again.

3. Abrahamic covenant

> Genesis 12:1-7
> Genesis 13:14-17
> Genesis 15:18-21
> Israel
> Unconditional

Israel is Gods people and He has promised them certain land. Today fighting still continues in Israel over land.

4. Palestinian covenant.

> Deuteronomy 30:1-10
>
> Israel
> Unconditional

It is a promise of land.

5. Mosaic covenant.

> Deuteronomy 1
> Exodus 19-20
> Israel
> Conditional

God says if you obey, I will bless you. If you disobey, I will punish you.

6. Davidic covenant.

    2 Samuel 7:8-16
    Israel
    Unconditional

Promise of a savior and a kingdom.

7. New Covenant

    Jeremiah 31:31-34
    Man, in general
    Unconditional

Promise of new relationship

In our texts today, primarily Jeremiah 30-33, the theme is a new covenant.

After several passages of gloom and judgement, these chapters provide hope and consolation.

As we read these chapters, we must keep in mind two applications:

1. They apply to Israel as promises of a return home. Remember, due to Israel's disobedience concerning the Sabbath, God raises up Assyria to capture the North in 722 B.C. and Babylon to capture the South in 586 B.C.

2. They also apply to the end of ages, the time of our Lord's return.

So, when reading these, one must be careful and determine whether the passage is:

- Talking only about Israel's return from captivity
- Talking about only the end of the age
- Or both

Let's keep the theme new and outline these chapters. Jeremiah 31:26 says he received this word in a dream. God would use dreams to speak to his servants.

How many of you dream? My wife dreams. As we are having our morning coffee at 4 or 5 a.m. she feels a need to share with me her dreams. I listen. She then asks me what does that mean? I mean, if God's preachers like Daniel and Jeremiah could interpret dreams, why shouldn't Mike Smith? Well, I can't.

So, as we get into these passages, Jeremiah 30-33, I am going to depend on God's word to interpret.

1. New Beginning – Jeremiah 30:1-24

Remember, the northern kingdom, Israel, was taken over by Assyria in 722 B.C. Judah, the southern kingdom, was taken over by Babylon in 586 B.C.

But the word of hope here is that they will eventually return to their land as a united people.

Jeremiah 30:3, "For, lo, the days come, saith the LORD, that I will bring again the captivity of my people Israel and Judah, saith the LORD: and I will cause them to return to the land that I gave to their fathers, and they shall possess it."

Remember, I said much of what these will apply is to the end of the age and to Israel now, both.

Jeremiah 30:3 references both.

Under Nehemiah, they would return. Also, at the end of the age Jews will return to Jerusalem. Since May 13, 1948, they have been returning.

Jeremiah uses another picture object lesson to teach us.

He uses ox and yoke. Vv. 4-11.

Jeremiah 30:8, "For it shall come to pass in that day, saith the LORD of hosts, that I will break his yoke from off thy neck, and will burst thy bonds, and strangers shall no more serve themselves of him:"

Look at the phrase "in that day." What is it referring to? Look back at Jeremiah 30:7. He talks of "time of Jacob's trouble."

This refers to 7 years of tribulation. Matthew 24:21-31; Mark 13:19-27; Revelation 6-19

Tribulation will be a time of suffering to get the Jews to turn to Jesus.

After the tribulation, God will judge these nations that have persecuted Israel.

God is the only one who can heal.

Calm after storm vv. 18-24

2. New People – Jeremiah 31:1-30

Here the emphasis is on a united people.

3. New Covenant – Jeremiah 31:31-40

Old covenant – outward – national – conduct - law

New Covenant – inward – personal – character – grac

4. New Land – Jeremiah 32:1-33

Another object lesson. Jeremiah is in prison. (37:21). Soon Jerusalem will fall. Here he tells Jeremiah to buy land.

Jeremiah 31:7 – Praise, Worship, Think about God

Jeremiah 31:7-8 – Prayer

Jeremiah 31:8-9 – Preserve

Verse 37 is a promise.

Look at Hebrews 10:36: "For ye have need of patience, that, after ye have done the will of God, ye might receive the promise."

Three lessons here:

- Trust
- Time – we have need of patience; we don't know God's timing; we want it now.
- Thrill – we might receive the promise.

God made a promise. I am going to give you the land.

Dr. Mike Smith

5

Collapse
Jeremiah 34-39

Judah is about to collapse. This great, glorious nation is about to die. This is the nation God has had His hand on. He led them out of Egypt. He gave them the promised land. They became the envy of all surrounding nations as their land prospered.

What caused this decay and final collapse?

- Historians will point to politics – depending on Egypt to protect them.
- Powerful leaders – making stupid decisions.
- Personal immorality and idolatry.

The cause of this collapse can be traced to the Word of God. Instead of looking to God they looked elsewhere for help.

This cannot be said only of an ancient nation. This can be said of an individual today. Let's learn from Judah's collapse.

1. God's word warns us – Jeremiah 34-35
   a. Setting – Jeremiah 34:1-7

The year was 588 B.C.

The Babylonian King Nebuchadnezzar had invaded Judah.

He had conquered all the major cities.

Only two remained.

Look at Jeremiah 34:7. They were Lachish, about 23 miles from Jerusalem, and Azekah, about 18 miles from Jerusalem. God sends his messenger Jeremiah to Judah's King Zedekiah. God is longsuffering and is going to give the king another chance to repent and do right.

Jeremiah warns Zedekiah that they would not escape judgement. He tells the king "You won't die but you will be taken captive."

   b. Sin – Jeremiah 34:8-22

Notice in 34:8-10. After the king hears his fate, he quickly makes a promise to God. I will release all the slaves.

Notice 34:11. The king breaks his promise and says to keep all the slaves.

Notice 34:12. God sends Jeremiah to remind King Zedekiah of the sin of Israel.

Verse 14 is clear: at the end of every seven years a slave was to be free. This was true of the land. Every seven years the land was to rest and not be planted.

This was all part of the Sabbath laws God had with Israel.

Look back.

Exodus 21:2, "If thou buy an Hebrew servant, six years he shall serve: and in the seventh he shall go out free for nothing."

Leviticus 25:4, "But in the seventh year shall be a sabbath of rest unto the land, a sabbath for the LORD: thou shalt neither sow thy field, nor prune thy vineyard."

God's people did not heed the warning and for 490 years they refused to rest their land on the seventh year. This was 70 Sabbaths. Thus, God sends them to Babylon for 70 years.

Leviticus 26:21 warns them, "And if ye walk contrary unto me, and will not hearken unto me; I will bring seven times more plagues upon you according to your sins."

You need to take God's Word seriously. It provides for us many wise warnings and we would do well to keep them. To disobey God is sin.

You cannot appease or manipulate God. A lot of people make what's often referred to as a foxhole promise. They are in trouble and they cry out to God, "If you will help me, I will give you 20%." God helps and they give him nothing.

That's like the man who falls off the roof. He cries out, "God, save me and I will serve you." About that time his pants get caught on a nail, and he stops falling and says, "that's ok, God, a nail caught me!"

God's word warns us.

Chapter 35 is like an illustration after a sermon. In Chapter 34, Jeremiah preaches, then in Chapter 35 he illustrates.

The illustration is at the house of the Rechabites. Rechabites were nomadic people. They had vowed not to drink wine. God tells Jeremiah to go to their house and set a bottle of wine in front of them, tempting them to drink. They refuse.

The lesson here is even these Rechabites are more faithful to their traditions than Judah was to God's Word.

2. God's word is wise and inspired – Jeremiah 36:1-32

Remember, the Bible was not written in chronological order. Jeremiah is not written in chronological order. Chapters 34-35 were written when Zedekiah was king in the 580's B.C. Now Chapter 36 is written in the fourth year of King Jehoiakin's reign in the 600's B.C.

a. Inspiration – Jeremiah 36:1-4

This is what we call inspiration. It means God breathes into. It is a picture of a mother hen hovering over her baby chicks. In inspiration, God the Holy Spirit, hovered over the human writers to assure that what we have is His word.

Notice here that God speaks to Jeremiah, and Jeremiah dictates to his secretary, Baruch, the Word of God. The Bible was written by 40 different authors over a period of 1,500 years. God allowed each writer to maintain his own style, personality, and vocabulary. He did not cause these men to be robot secretaries writing as He dictates. Yet in this freedom, He hovers over them to assure that what we have is what He intended us to have.

b. Proclamation – Jeremiah 36:5-26

Jeremiah isn't allowed to go to the temple. So, he sends Baruch. He proclaims the word. Romans 10:14, "How shall they hear without a preacher?" Notice the response to the word being read.

• Curiosity – v. 11-15

This man, Micaiah, was concerned about what he heard. Micaiah was the grandson of Shaphan, the man who read the lost book to King Josiah (2 Kings 22). So, it is no wonder he had an interest or curiosity.

• Conviction or Concern – Jeremiah 36:16-20

They read the book to the leaders and we see fear or concern when the people read the word. The Holy Spirit will bring them under conviction that often results in fear or concern.

• Cover Up – Jeremiah 36:21-26

Jehudi, probably one of the scribes or secretaries, took it to the king and read it. The king treated it as fuel for the fire and burned the Word of God.

• Continuation of God's Word – Jeremiah 36:27-32

Down through time, men have tried to destroy God's word but have failed. We have this promise in in Isaiah 40:8, "The grass withereth, the flower fadeth: but the word of our God shall stand for ever." And 1 Peter 1:24-25, "For all flesh is as grass, and all the glory of man as the flower of grass. The grass withereth, and the flower thereof falleth away: But the word of the LORD endureth for ever. And this is the word which by the gospel is preached unto you."

God simply told Jeremiah to write it again.

By the way, Jehoiakim did not last long after that. Then his son, Jehoiachin, only lasted 3 months.

3. God's Word is Without Honor – Jeremiah 37-38

Notice the way Zedekiah treats God's word. He is so fickle. He is so vacillating. Indecision will kill you.

Jeremiah 37:3 – Pray for us. It is like King Zedekiah said, "just in case Jeremiah is right and there is a God, will you pray for us?"

The king's men were afraid of Jeremiah in 37:15 and put him in prison after beating him. The prayer wasn't being answered. Nebuchadnezzar kept marching toward Jerusalem.

If someone asks you to pray for them and they don't get the answer they wanted, be careful.

Jeremiah 37:17b says yes, "I have a word; you are going to be made a prisoner of the King of Babylon." Zedekiah did not like that answer.

Chapter 38 is the scene where Zedekiah officials were angry and Jeremiah's words and wanted to kill him. Verse 4 says "...let this man be put to death...."

4. God's Word with Honor – Jeremiah 39

Jeremiah 39:1, "In the ninth year of Zedekiah king of Judah, in the tenth month, came Nebuchadnezzar, king of Babylon, and all his army against Jerusalem, and they besieged it."

January 15, 588, and two years later, July 18, 586, the Babylonians took over Jerusalem.

Zedekiah and his family are caught. Zedekiah's family is killed. Zedekiah is taken prisoner. Verse 14 – Nebuchadnezzar has Jeremiah taken out of prison.

Look at 39:17-18, "But I will deliver thee in that day, saith the LORD: and thou shalt not be given into the hand of the men of whom thou art afraid. For I will surely deliver thee, and thou shalt not fall by the sword, but thy life shall be for a prey unto thee: because thou hast put thy trust in me, saith the LORD."

God's word is true and with honor.

CONCLUSION

I lived in the 1960-70's, during the battle of conservative resurgence. Our Baptist schools were drifting into liberalism. I believe there had to be correction.

Now I see another drifting of the word. It concerns me. People will say they believe God's word, but they live and obey only the parts they want to.

We need to honor the word or there will be a collapse.

6

Countries
Jeremiah 40-49

Billy Graham was born on November 7, 1918, in North Carolina. He died February 21, 2018, at home in Montreat, North Carolina. Listen to some facts about his life:

- 2.2 Billion heard him preach.
- 215 Million heard him live.
- 2.2 Million responded to invitations.
- 185 Nations
- 13 Presidents from Harry Truman to Barack Obama invited him to pray for them (facts and trends.com)

He was not only America's preacher, but the most well-known preacher to all nations.

Jeremiah was noted for being a prophet to the nations. In chapters 40-49, we get a glimpse of his life and message. Just as we can learn much from others, let's review the life of Jeremiah.

Jeremiah 40 is similar to the account in Jeremiah 39. The scene is that Nebuchadnezzar, King of Babylon, had made three invasions into Israel. He was taking key people back to Babylon. Scripture says he took the best looking and smartest captive. I tell my students, if Babylon invades Jacksonville, don't worry, they won't take you!

When Nebuchadnezzar invades Israel, Jeremiah is in prison. He is released. He is given an option to go to Babylon or stay in Jerusalem. For him to be invited to go to Babylon would have been the easiest path, but he chooses to stay in the land with the people that were left.

Ezekiel becomes a preacher to those in Babylon.

What can we learn from Jeremiah?

1. Jeremiah is a pastor.

Jeremiah 40:4 records how he could have gone to Babylon and had a cushy job. He chose to stay with the remnant. Why? He was a pastor at heart.

This is a true pastor. He has a heart of love for his people.

Sometimes a preacher will make a joke or statement trying to be funny. They say: pastoring would be great if it weren't for the people. What?

Pastors are to be in the people business. If you don't like people, quit and get into another line of work. Jeremiah was a pastor for he wanted to be with his people.

2. Jeremiah is protected.

Nebuchadnezzar appointed Gedaliah as governor over Israel as he went back to Babylon. Jeremiah 40:7, "Now when all the captains of the forces which were in the fields, even they and their men, heard that the king of Babylon had made Gedaliah the son of Ahikam governor in the land, and had committed unto him men, and women, and children, and of the poor of the land, of them that were not carried away captive to Babylon."

In Chapter 40, you see a lot of killing going on. Gedeliah is governor. He is naïve.

We see in Verse 14, Ishmael plots to and succeeds in killing him. Then Johanan plots to kill Ishmael. In all this killing they are jockeying for power of Jerusalem. God protects Jeremiah.

When you do and be what God wants, you are in the safest place. If God calls you to go to North Korea on a mission trip, it will be safer there in obedience than here in Texas in disobedience. The safest place in the world to be is in the will of God. The most dangerous place to be in the world is to be out of God's will.

3. Jeremiah is a prayer warrior.

Jeremiah 42:1-3, "Then all the captains of the forces, and Johanan the son of Kareah, and Jezaniah the son of Hoshaiah, and all the people from the least even unto the greatest, came near, And said unto Jeremiah the prophet, Let, we beseech thee, our supplication be accepted before thee, and pray for us unto the LORD thy God, even for all this remnant; (for we are left but a few of many, as thine eyes do behold us:) That the LORD thy God may shew us the way wherein we may walk, and the thing that we may do."

Those who were left in Jerusalem came to Jeremiah and asked for prayer. Look at 42:4. Jeremiah says okay, you ask me to pray for you and I will, but I am going to tell you I will hold nothing back. Whatever God says this I will declare. It was not the kind of prayer of patting them on the back and saying, I will pray for you and everything is going to be all right. Some asking for prayers had not been believers.

Reminds me of a story of a woman who lived next door to an atheist. She was always trying to witness to the atheist and she often would tell the atheist she was praying for him. One day the woman ran out of food and she knelt down and asked God for food. The atheist overheard here and went to the grocery store and bought her groceries. He put the food on her porch and hid out. The woman came out and saw the food and prayed, "Praise God, my prayer has been answered." The atheist stepped out from hiding and said "Woman, God didn't buy those groceries, I did." The woman bowed her head and prayed, "God, thank you for providing the food and having the devil to pay for it."

4. Jeremiah is a preacher

Chapter 44:1, "The word that came to Jeremiah concerning all the Jews which dwell in the land of Egypt, which dwell at Migdol, and at Tahpanhes, and at Noph, and in the country of Pathros, saying,"

Here we see Jeremiah the preacher. Throughout the book of Jeremiah, he has proclaimed God's word. He was not popular, but he was obedient to God.

Look at 44:15-16, "Then all the men which knew that their wives had burned incense unto other gods, and all the women that stood by, a great multitude, even all the people that dwelt in the land of Egypt, in Pathros, answered Jeremiah, saying, As for the word that thou hast spoken unto us in the name of the LORD, we will not hearken unto thee."

They openly and blatantly said, God we are not going to do what you say. When Jeremiah preached, the people did not listen.

Then they said, look Jeremiah, this works for us. Some were worshipping the Queen of Heaven. They prospered so they thought they were better off with their god instead of Jeremiah's God.

5. Jeremiah the Prophet

In Jeremiah 45-49 we see Jeremiah the prophet. Look at 45:1, "The word that Jeremiah the prophet spake unto Baruch the son of Neriah, when he had written these words in a book at the mouth of Jeremiah, in the fourth year of Jehoiakim the son of Josiah king of Judah, saying,

Remember Baruch, Jeremiah's secretary. He seems discouraged. So, in this short chapter, the prophet tries to bring encouragement.

Every prophet in the Bible has a message of judgment and comfort. Jeremiah was faithful to preach what God said. Often that was a message of judgment. But he was also a preacher of encouragement.

Jeremiah preached for over 40 years and people would not listen. Now God gives him a message to those nations connected to Israel. Look back in Jeremiah 1:5, "Before I formed thee in the belly I knew thee; and before thou camest forth out of the womb I sanctified thee, and I ordained thee a prophet unto the nations."

He was called to be a prophet to the nations and now we see this come true.

1. Egypt – 46:1-28

Egyptian Pharaoh Necho had defeated Judah and killed King Josiah at Megiddo in 609 (2 Chronicles 35:20-27) but now when Nebuchadnezzar invades Judah, the Egyptians leave.

Jeremiah 46:25-26, "The LORD of hosts, the God of Israel, saith; Behold, I will punish the multitude of No, and Pharaoh, and Egypt, with their gods, and their kings; even Pharaoh, and all them that trust in him: And I will deliver them into the hand of those that seek their lives, and into the hand of Nebuchadrezzar king of Babylon, and into the hand of his servants: and afterward it shall be inhabited, as in the days of old, saith the LORD."

2. Philistia – 47:1-7

Jeremiah uses word pictures of a rising flooded river to describe how the Babylonian army would come in and take over nations.

3. Moab – 48:1-47

Moabites were descendants of Lot. They were Judah's enemy. In 582 Nebuchadnezzar's army invaded Moab and destroyed them.

Look at Jeremiah 48:7, "For because thou hast trusted in thy works and in thy treasures, thou shalt also be taken: and Chemosh shall go forth into captivity with his priests and his princes together."

This was a judgment on their pride.

4. Ammon – 49:1-6

Ammonites were another product of Lot's incestuous union with his daughters.

They thought they were safe because of their position. They were surrounded by mountains. But when God decrees a judgment, nothing can protect them.

5. Edom – 49:7-22

Edomites were descendants of Jacob's brother Esau. They were the Jews' enemy. Edom's judgment is described like a harvest where nothing is left.

6. Syria – 49:23-27

Jeremiah predicts as Babylon invades, they will become weak and sick.

7. Kedar and Hazo – 49:28-33

These are desert people. Kedar was related to Ishmael. They were nomadic sheep herders. Nebuchadnezzar attacked them in 599. They were guilty of living the easy life and not fearing anyone. When Nebuchadnezzar came to town, they saw how foolish they had been.

8. Elam – 49:34-39

Elamites were Semitic people who were Babylonia's neighbors. They were known for their archery. So, God promised to break their bows in Jeremiah 49:35, "Thus saith the LORD of hosts; Behold, I will break the bow of Elam, the chief of their might."

CONCLUSION

Hebrews 10:31 reminds us, "It is a fearful thing to fall into the hands of the living God."

7

Conclusion
Jeremiah 50-52

Have you ever heard the phrase "what goes around comes around?" This fits Babylon. Babylon has bullied the nations of the word, particularly, Israel as described in the whole book of Jeremiah. Now in Jeremiah 50-51, we see they get what they deserve.

In scripture, Babylon has always stood for evil and the opposite of good in Jerusalem.

Babylon was the proud city of man.

Jerusalem was the holy city of God.

The word babel means confusion. Remember the Tower of Babel in Genesis 11. God confused the human languages. The founder was Nimrod, a mighty hunter or rebel against God. Babylon is a symbol of rebellion against God. In Revelation 17-18, she is portrayed as a great prostitute.

Jeremiah was told to preach the fall of Babylon. Jeremiah 50:1-3, "The word that the LORD spake against Babylon and against the land of the Chaldeans by Jeremiah the prophet. Declare ye among the nations, and publish, and set up a standard; publish, and conceal not: say, Babylon is taken, Bel is confounded, Merodach is broken in pieces; her idols are confounded, her images are broken in pieces. For out of the north there cometh up a nation against her, which shall make her land desolate, and none shall dwell therein: they shall remove, they shall depart, both man and beast."

Babylon fell in 539 at the hands of the Persian leader, Cyrus.

The fall of Babylon is a story of victory. It meant the salvation of God's people.

In this story, we see a parallel to our victory or blessings in salvation.

1. Redemption – 50:34
   a. The fall of Babylon is one of two great stories of redemption in the Old Testament. The first was Exodus when God brought Israel out of bondage in Egypt.
   b. The second is here, with the fall of Babylon. God brings his people out of slavery back home to Jerusalem.
   c. Look at verse 50:33. They held Israel and refused to let them go. But God is our Redeemer. Christ is our Redeemer. As a lost person, I was in slavery to sin. I was estranged or separated from God. Jesus came, died on the cross, shed his blood, and paid the price of my sin. His redemption brought me back to God. I Peter 1:18-19, "Forasmuch as ye know that ye were not redeemed with corruptible things, as silver and gold, from your vain conversation received by tradition from your fathers; But with the precious blood of Christ, as of a lamb without blemish and without spot:"

2. Repentance – 50:4

   a. When God redeemed the Jews, they did not just go back to Jerusalem, they went back to God. After 70 years away from Jerusalem, they became aware of the price of sin and separation from God. Repentance is often accompanied with tears of sorrow.

3. Renewal of covenant – 50:5

   a. The Jews were bound to God by a covenant or contract. As Christians, we are bound to God by a covenant.

4. Return by the Shepherd – 50:6-7; 50:17-19

Israel had been lost sheep. Their shepherds had led them astray. Jeremiah, throughout the book, told us of bad shepherds. Jeremiah 10:21, "For the pastors are become brutish, and have not sought the LORD: therefore, they shall not prosper, and all their flocks shall be scattered." Jeremiah 23:1, "Woe be unto the pastors that destroy and scatter the sheep of my pasture! saith the LORD."

Assyria conquered the northern tribes in 722 and led them away in 610. But God punished Assyria with Babylon and now God promises to punish Babylon and lead Israel back and feed them.

5. Reserve and forgive by atonement – 50:20

Throughout Jeremiah, he had vividly described the sin of Israel and Judah - adultery, idolatry, lying, cheating, and on and on. Now he reminds us he had forgiven

This is what Jesus did on the cross. All of our sins were forgiven by the death of Christ.

Jeremiah 51 is a repeat of chapter 50.

Jeremiah 52 seems out of place. Some will say it falls with Jeremiah 37.

But in conclusion, Jeremiah gives us the theme of most prophets, that of judgment and hope. Jeremiah 51:2 is a judgment on King Zedekiah. Starting in 588 B.C. (Jeremiah 52:4) and ending with the fall of Jerusalem in 586 B.C., the time of the Gentiles had begun (Luke 21:24). Zedekiah and his family tried to escape but were caught and taken to Babylon, where he died. That was judgment. But we see hope.

In Jeremiah 52:31-34, King Jehoiachin had been in prison for 3 years. Now he is released and trades his prison clothes for a royal robe. This is important. Why? He is David's rightful heir. God had promised to put a son of David on the throne. Jeremiah 23:5, 6; 30:8; 33:14-17. The end of the book of Jeremiah gives us hope. There is a king to save his people.

The sequel or rest of the story is found in Matthew 1:12-16:

- Jehoiachin was the father of Shealtiel
- Shealtiel was the father of Zerubbabel
- Zerubbabel was the father of Abiud
- Abiud was the father of Eliakin
- Eliakin was the father of Azor
- Azor was the father of Zadok
- Zadok was the father of Achin
- Achin was the father of Eliud
- Eliud was the father of Eleazar
- Eleazar was the father of Matthen
- Matthen was the father of Jacob
- Jacob was the father of Joseph.
- Joseph was the husband of Mary, of whom Jesus was born.

8

What We Learn from Jeremiah

Jeremiah was one of the outstanding Old Testament prophets. His unique style continues to captivate hearts and minds today. The teaching in his book is rich with meaning and its application when heeded makes our lives richer. Here are a few of the highlights.

1. God takes sin seriously. They broke the Sabbath. So what? Times are hard and everyone is doing it. 70 years in captivity.

2. God's word is to be taken seriously. We see over and over God's prophet preaching and people just keep right on sinning. Because they resist God's word, they suffer. Today many lives suffer for not taking God's word seriously.

3. God calls faithfulness a success. By today's standards, Jeremiah was a failure. He preached for 40 years and really had no followers. 1 Corinthians 4:2, "Moreover it is required in stewards, that a man be found faithful."

So, this says, "preachers, don't quit. Keep on preaching." Someone has said, "it's always too soon to quit."
4. God will settle all accounts. Sin will be judged. The nations who have bullied Israel will pay, have paid, and will face a judgment.
5. God wants us to live in hope and share that hope – Jesus.

In Matthew 16:13-14, "When Jesus came into the coasts of Caesarea Philippi, he asked his disciples, saying, Whom do men say that I the Son of man am? And they said, Some say that thou art John the Baptist: some, Elias; and others, Jeremias, or one of the prophets."

- Jeremiah was like Jesus.
- He was a type.
- Both were single.
- Both were rejected by their hometown.
- Both were accused of being traitors.
- Both emphasized heart religion rather than traditions.
- Both were considered a failure.

But that is quite an honor to be compared to Jesus.

Sermons from Jeremiah

4 Then the word of the LORD came unto me, saying,
5 Before I formed thee in the belly I knew thee; and
before thou camest forth out of the womb I sanctified
thee, and I ordained thee a prophet unto the nations.
6 Then said I, Ah, Lord GOD! behold, I cannot speak:
for I am a child.
7 But the LORD said unto me, Say not, I am a child:
for thou shalt go to all that I shall send thee, and
whatsoever I command thee thou shalt speak.
8 Be not afraid of their faces: for I am with thee to
deliver thee, saith the LORD.

Jeremiah 1:4-8 (KJV)

1 I charge thee therefore before God, and the Lord
Jesus Christ, who shall judge the quick and the dead at
his appearing and his kingdom;
2 Preach the word; be instant in season, out of season;
reprove, rebuke, exhort with all longsuffering and
doctrine.

2 Timothy 4:1-2 (KJV)

Sermon 1

First Person Overview of Jeremiah's Life

Good evening. I am Jeremiah, God's prophet to Judah. My name Yirmeyahu means Jehovah touches. Truly the touch of God has been upon my life.

I was born in a small, poor village called Anathoth, 3 miles north of Jerusalem. My father, Hilkiah, was a Jewish priest.

When I was born, Manasseh was king. Manasseh was Judah's worst king. The country was in a terrible condition. False idols were erected everywhere. Murder, adultery, and idolatry filled the air. Babies were offered as sacrifices, thrown into open fires. Children were taught to gather wood and offer drink offering sacrifices to false gods. The Temple, God's house, was made into a headquarters of Baal worship.

In such a wicked day, I lived.

In the year 626 B.C., God touched my life and called me to preach. I was just a young man.

I was scared when God called me for I was

- Not as mighty as Elijah
- Not as eloquent at Isaiah
- Not as angelic as Ezekiel

But God said, "before I formed thee in the belly I knew you and before you were born I ordained you to preach." I said, "God, I can't speak." God said, "Be not afraid, for I am with you." Then the LORD put forth his hand and touched my mouth and said, "Behold, I have put my words in thy mouth."

With the touch of God's hand, I began to speak for God.

I preached during the reign of 5 Hebrew kings from 626 B.C. to the fall of Jerusalem in 586 B.C.

I started preaching when Josiah was king (640-609 B.C.). He was a good king. He ordered the Temple repaired and false gods thrown out. It was while he was king that the book of Deuteronomy was found in the Temple.

In 609, Josiah was killed at Megiddo by Necho of Egypt.

His son, Jehoahaz, became king. He ruled only 3 months, then Necho of Egypt deported him in chains.

Jehoiakim was the next king (609-597 B.C.). He was a godless, evil king. Once while I was dictating God's word to my secretary, Baruch, Jehoiakim took the scroll and burned it.

In 597 B.C. the Babylonians defeated the Egyptians and took over Palestine. Jehoiakin sided with the Babylonians. I warned him against this. Soon after, Jehoiakim was mysteriously found dead.

Jehoiachin was the next king in 597 B.C., but he lasted only 3 months before he and 10,000 of our leading citizens of Jerusalem, like Daniel, were taken captive to Babylon.

The last king was Zedekiah in 597 B.C. He ruled during the time Jerusalem was captured and until it was destroyed by Nebuchadnezzar.

Gedaliah was made a puppet governor over Judah but was soon assassinated.

I lived to see my nation go down into sin, war, and judgement.

Some of you here tonight can understand what I feel. For you have seen your nation, America, fall into sin, war, and only by God's grace judgement has not come. Some of you have seen your family turn from God and fall under the judgement of sin. You know how my heart aches. That's why I was called by some "The Weeping Prophet."

My preaching was a dramatic style of preaching like I am doing tonight before you. God told me to do some unusual things to visualize my message.

I've experienced a lot in my life, like many of you. I want to review some of my life as found in the book that bears my name, and possibly relate to your life.

When a generation refuses to hear God's word, the time comes when God often uses the unusual, out of the ordinary, means to speak to man.

God had me do some unusual things to visualize his word to the people.

Let me share some of these unusual things.

CHAPTER 7

One day, God told me to go to the gate of the Temple, the very center of worship, and preach "amend your ways."

This seemed strange to tell the people as they were coming into church to "straighten up your life."

But you see, the people thought as long as they came to church every week and stayed religiously active everything would be okay.

God said "I don't want you to be religiously active but righteously obedient. I want you to clean up your life". The people were so bad, God told me not to pray for them and he said if you do, I will not hear.

People, it is dangerous, year after year, month after month, week after week, to come to church and not get right with God. Listen, God looks at your life, not your 30 years of Sunday School attendance.

Don't get so caught up in religious activity that you cannot hear God, or worse, that God won't hear you.

CHAPTER 13

One day, God told me to put on a lion's girdle. This was a priest's cloth or a symbol of service. I was to wear this and not wash it day after day, all over Jerusalem. This was to remind the people they were to be servants.

Then God told me to bury it 400 miles away along the Euphrates River. It took me 3 months to travel there to bury it and 3 months to travel back.

Then God told me to go back and dig up the cloth and wear it. The cloth was rotten and useless.

This was a message to the people that unless they served God, they would become useless.

There are a lot of good things you can give your life to. Family, clubs, gardening, nice lawns, beautiful flowers, a big house, trips, but don't be like people of my day, that you get to a place in life where your life is like old, rotten material, useless to God.

CHAPTER 16

Chapter 16 of my book records how, when everyone else was marrying and having children, God told me not to marry nor have children. Part of the reason was during this time Nebuchadnezzar was taking children and beating their heads against rocks. God wanted to spare me the anguish. Under certain circumstances, it is best not to get married and not have children.

Some of you here may be single, wanting, looking forward, seeking, praying and fasting, to get married. Fine, if it is God's plan. But like me – Jeremiah, God said it is best not to and maybe you have received such a word from God.

CHAPTER 35

On one occasion, God told me to go to the house of the Rechabites. These were nomadic people who did not drink wine, did not build house nor plant crops, but lived in tents.

I was told to set before them wine to drink.

This was not to tempt them to sin, but to demonstrate to Judah how these Rechabites were more faithful to their earthly fathers in not drinking wine than Judah had been to their heavenly father. There are those who live by tradition because it is simple, clear-cut, and it is definite. Such a life demands no soul-searching, fasting or prayers, just do the same old thing day in and day out. See, it is much easier to do what someone else thinks you ought to do than finding out what God wants you to do.

Some of you may be in comfortable retirement, living life the way your children, friends, family, think you ought to live. But I ask you, are you living the way God wants you to live? Oh, don't misunderstand. I was not always roaring, busting, going all out for God.

Chapter 9 records a time I told God – I am ready to give up. Let me have a nice cabin in the desert all alone.

Then God reminded me of the call from within of his plan for my life and of the call from without of the need to warn others.

You may be here tonight, ready to give up. Saying just leave me alone, preacher, I have my nest arranged and don't disturb me. Remember God's will and plan for your life. Five different times I was thrown into prison. One time I was thrown into an old dungeon. It was the evil ruler's way of saying I don't want to hear from you. You are causing too much trouble. Just go into prison and plan to die.

You know what God tome me as recorded in Chapter 32 and 33? To buy land from my cousin. At the darkest day in my life, in the darkest day of Judah's life, when everyone else was selling, God told me to buy land. Why? To show everyone that He is in control and that there will be a tomorrow and the sun will shine.

Some people may be trying to get you to sell out, give up, do nothing, keep quiet.

You listen to God!

My favorite lesson God taught me in an unusual way took place at the Potter's house. Chapters 18 & 19 records this.

I just watched the potter make a vessel out of a lump of clay.

A.   This taught me how God has power over our lives.

God is a big God. He can do anything he so wills. As I watched, I noticed the potter was purposefully making a vessel. I was not sure what he was making at first, but he had a picture in his mind. This reminded me that:

B.   God has a plan for each of us.

God is not fooling around; He is purposefully working in our lives to accomplish His purpose. It is reassuring to know in the midst of life's problems, pressures, and perplexities, God is in control and He is purposefully at work.

Then I noticed the potter fund a marred piece of hard clay in his lump and took it out.

This taught me that in many of our lives there is hardness – hard, non-pliable areas – that God needs to remove.

Tonight, in your life, there may be a hardness that is making it difficult for God to work his work in your life

I watched as the potter took the hardness out and remade the vessel.

This reminded me how a lot of Christians need to be reworked by God.

A fresh touch from Him, a redirection to get back on course.

Revival is a renewal, a new work of God in your life.

Jeremiah's commission was:

A. Dangerous

He lived in a very pagan world. Notice in Verse 10 his job description:

Pluck up – He was to uproot idol worship.

Breakdown – Tear down false structures of society

Destroy – Means do away with corruption

Overthrow – Means to demolish

It is very difficult to be an upstream Christian in a downstream world. Our society is trying to move everyone away from God. Our services as Christians is to move them toward God. It is an uphill battle.

Even among church people, the cry is for tolerance, acceptance, love and forgiveness. The church is too silent on sin. We want everyone to love one another and just get along. People, we need to wake up. We need to get busy proclaiming the gospel to the nations. We need to walk across the street, and we need to go across the ocean.

Judgment is coming. I feel America is boiling. I have never seen so much anger and hatred in my lifetime. Judgment is coming.

God's words to Jeremiah talks of a war. I mean pluck up, tear down, demolish does not sound like kum bay a. Let's all get together.

B. Depressing

Jeremiah's commission was depressing. 50 years he preached, cried, called for repentance. Yet there was not one single convert that we know of.

God ends chapter one with 3 object lessons to give him hope.

1. Almond tree – Verse 11

This tree was the first to bloom in spring. It was a promise of life to come.

2. Boiling Pot – Verse 13

This speaks of judgment and cleaning.

3. Iron Pillar – Verse 18

God will provide strength.

Jeremiah had to do some strange things. But it all starts with giving your life to Jesus and letting him be in control every day, not just one day a week, but every day.

You can start right now, right here, letting Jesus be in control.

You can go home, go back to school, and let Jesus be in control.

Sermon 2

The Touch of the Master's Hand
Jeremiah 18:1-10, 19:10-11

INTRODUCTION

I pastored First Baptist Church of Edom for three years, as some of you know. Most of you know that Edom is well known for its annual Edom arts and craft fair held every September, attracting thousand from all over East Texas. This festival is sponsored by the Edom Crafts Association. Several years ago, a group of artisans moved into the old vacant business in Edom and established their craft stores. If you have driven through downtown Edom, you've noticed the knife maker, silversmith, leather works, and the potter's shop. Potter Brown's shop was my favorite. Often while I was filling up with gas, I would just browse around his shop and watch him work the clay on the potter's wheel. It fascinated me the way Potter Brown could take a hunk of clay and shape it into a beautiful vase, bowl, pitcher, cup, or plates.

God told Jeremiah to go to a potter's house one day. Jeremiah 18:1-10 records that experience of Jeremiah at the potter's house.

Turn there if you will.

Sunday, we looked at Hebrews 10 & 11 about Abram's life and saw if we were to have revival we need to return to faith – simply trusting and obeying God. To believe he could do it. He could reach that hard heart.

Monday, we looked at Numbers 32:23 and saw that if we were to have revival, we had to deal with sin for truly your sins will find you out.

Tonight, we will look in Jeremiah 18:1-10 and we will see if we are to have revival, we must yield our lives to God and allow Him to change us to His way.

Have you ever wished you could start over? Have you ever wished your life could be different from what it is?

Jeremiah gives us hope at this point in the potter's house in Jeremiah 18:1-10.

1 The word which came to Jeremiah from the LORD, saying,
2 Arise, and go down to the potter's house, and there I will cause thee to hear my words.
3 Then I went down to the potter's house, and, behold, he wrought a work on the wheels.
4 And the vessel that he made of clay was marred in the hand of the potter: so he made it again another vessel, as seemed good to the potter to make it.
5 Then the word of the LORD came to me, saying,
6 O house of Israel, cannot I do with you as this potter? saith the LORD. Behold, as the clay is in the potter's hand, so are ye in mine hand, O house of Israel.
7 At what instant I shall speak concerning a nation, and concerning a kingdom, to pluck up, and to pull down, and to destroy it;
8 If that nation, against whom I have pronounced, turn from their evil, I will repent of the evil that I thought to do unto them.

9 And at what instant I shall speak concerning a nation, and concerning a kingdom, to build and to plant it; 10 If it do evil in my sight, that it obey not my voice, then I will repent of the good, wherewith I said I would benefit them.

Jeremiah is one of the most interesting prophets. He was born at Anathoth, a small village six miles north of Jerusalem. He prophesied during the reign of four Hebrew Kings, from 626 B.C. to the fall of Jerusalem in 586 B.C.

One day the Lord told him to go to the potter's house and there he would hear the message he was to preach.

As Jeremiah watched the potter at work, the Lord gave him a message into how God deals with man. Let's look at this message.

I.   The Divine Potter God has power over human clay.

Notice verse 6 "...Behold, as the clay is in the potter's hand, so are ye in mine hand..."

Jeremiah saw the sovereignty of God. Listen to this. God is in charge, He rules, He still has a way in what goes on. God is a big God.

This humanist man-centered philosophy that is being expounded today is sickening. To say God is sovereign is to say, "...for all that is in the heaven and in the earth is thine..." 1 Chronicles 29:11. To say God is sovereign is to declare with Psalm 115:3, "But our God is in the heavens: he hath done whatsoever he hath pleased."

To say God is sovereign is to declare He is the, "...only Potentate, the King of kings, and LORD of Lords;"

God could, this moment, make the Rockies into the swamps of Louisiana and the swamps of Louisiana the Rockies.

God is sovereign.

One day God had a job for Moses. He needed to persuade Moses that He was God and had the power to do it.

So, he said to Moses, what's that in your hand and Moses replied, a rod.

Moses was probably surprised that God noticed such a small thing. God told Moses to put the rod down. Moses did, and it became a hissing, wiggling snake.

Then God told Moses to pick it up. Now I don't believe it was that hard to lay down the rod but to pick it up was a different matter. Yet Moses picked it up and the snake became a rod again.

God was trying to teach Moses "Look, I am sovereign, I am in charge, I am a big God."

God may be trying to teach you tonight that same lesson, that he is a big God and He has power.

It might be tonight that God is trying to get you to lay down that ugly habit, that hot temper, that critical spirit, that secret sin, that indifferent and negative attitude, and let God do a work in your life.

God can change your life. No matter how sinful you feel, how worthless, how useless, how inadequate, God can change your life. God is a God of power.

II.   *The Divine Potter God has a plan for your life.*

Notice verse 3, "he wrought a work on the wheels." God has a plan for your life.

Just as every potter that sits at a potter's wheel with a hunk of clay has a plan for that clay, God has a plan for your life.

John 15:16 says, "Ye have not chosen me, but I have chosen you, and ordained you, that ye should go and bring forth fruit..."

God is not playing around. You are not some toy in His hand. God has a purpose and plan for your life.

God means to do something with your life.

You are special to God.

One day while visiting the jail in Canton, I noticed on the wall a picture of a little boy and saying by his picture. It said, "I am special cause God don't make no junk."

You are special to God.

I used to get so mad at school when I was in class and we had to number off every day to check attendance. That's all we were to them, just a number. Some days I wanted to stand up and say, I am not 86 but I am Mike Smith.

Our world is growing less and less personal with computers. While in Brussels, Belgium, recently, I got a taxi and asked to go to the common market. There at this huge building I was told they had a computer that occupied 3 stories and they had everyone down with a number.

The world is growing less and less personal and you may be just a number to the world, but not with God.

God knows you inside and out.

He knows the sparrow that falls to the ground. He knows the hairs upon your head. God knows you and cares for you. He has a plan for you.

All through the Bible we see how God has a plan for our lives.

Take a little 12-year-old shepherd boy who was called to kill a giant and become a king.

Take a young hot head rebel who was on the way to kill Christians when God blinded him and turned him around to become a great missionary and write half of the New Testament.

God has a plan for you.

The greatest place in the world to be is in God's plan.

III.   The Divine Potter God sees marred vessels.

Look at verse 4, "And the vessel that he made of clay was marred in the hand of the potter..."

Why is it that some vessels do not turn out to be beautiful works and usable objects?

Is it because the potter is unskilled?

No, it is because something goes wrong with the clay. It usually develops a hardness that makes it unworkable.

God is sovereign, He is all-powerful. God does have a plan for your life.

Do you know the one thing that can delay or hinder that plan?

SIN.

Sin is a hardness of the heart. A rebellious spirit. A desire to do it your way instead of God's way.

God has created each and every one of you here.

God has a plan for you.

If you are lost here tonight, then you need to realize it is your sin that is separating you from God and keeping you from fulfilling His plan for your life.

You need to deal with the sin in your heart by turning from it and coming to Christ, who can forgive you of your sin.

If you are saved here tonight but have little or no direction or purpose in life, then it could be unconfessed sin in your life and your life is thwarted by that sin.

Psalm 66:18, "If I regard iniquity in my heart, the LORD will not hear me:"

That means to hold on to sin and not confess it is to hinder you finding and fulfilling God's will for your life.

Let me share with you the lives of two men who lived in the 1700's.

ONE WAS A BELIEVER JONATHAN EDWARDS	THE OTHER WAS AN UNBELIEVER MAX JUTES
Edwards married a believer	Jutes married an unbeliever
Edwards had 729 descendants	Jutes had 1,026 descendants
Edwards descendants were:	Jutes descendants were:
300 Ministers	300 Died early
65 College Professors	100 Went to prison
13 University Professors	200 Prostitutes
3 U. S. Congressmen	100 Alcoholics
1 Vice President	

Sin will mar your life and keep you from finding God's will for your life.

IV. *The Divine Potter God makes another vessel.*

Notice verse 4, "...he made it again another vessel..."

Man can resist the will of God. The Bible states "all have sinned and come short of the glory of God."

But in Christ we can become new creatures.

2 Corinthians 5:17, "Therefore if any man be in Christ, he is a new creature: old things are passed away; behold, all things are become new."

So tonight, no matter how marred, sinful, or scarred your life is, if you will come to Christ, He can make you a new vessel.

Now don't put it off. If sin is in your life, deal with it and get your life in line with God's will for it.

For the 19ᵗʰ chapter, verses 10-11 warns there comes a time of hardening when the vessel cannot be made whole again.

Don't delay.

Come to Jesus and confess your sin and let him shape your life into the vessel that will honor and please him.

THE TOUCH OF THE MASTER'S HAND

'Twas battered and scarred, and the auctioneer
    Thought it scarcely worth his while
To waste much time on the old violin,
    But held it up with a smile.
"What am I bidden, good folks," he cried,
    "Who'll start the bidding for me?"
"A dollar, a dollar. Then two! Only two?
    Two dollars, and who'll make it three?"

"Three dollars, once; three dollars, twice;
    Going for three..." But no,
From the room, far back, a grey-haired man
    Came forward and picked up the bow;
Then wiping the dust from the old violin,
    And tightening the loosened strings,
He played a melody pure and sweet,
    As a caroling angel sings.

The music ceased, and the auctioneer,
    With a voice that was quiet and low,
Said: "What am I bid for the old violin?"
    And he held it up with the bow.

"A thousand dollars, and who'll make it two?
Two thousand! And who'll make it three?
Three thousand, once; three thousand, twice,
And going and gone," said he.

The people cheered, but some of them cried,
"We do not quite understand.
What changed its worth?" Swift came the reply:
"The touch of the Master's hand."
And many a man with life out of tune,
And battered and scarred with sin,
Is auctioned cheap to the thoughtless crowd
Much like the old violin.

A "mess of pottage," a glass of wine,
A game — and he travels on.
He is "going" once, and "going" twice,
He's "going" and almost "gone."
But the Master comes, and the foolish crowd
Never can quite understand
The worth of a soul and the change that is wrought
By the touch of the Master's hand.
(Myra Brooks Welch)

CONCLUSION

Have you ever experienced the touch of the Master's hand?

Jeremiah 18 & 19 – Touch of Master's Hand

Sermon 3

Do You Ever Feel Like Quitting?
Jeremiah 9:2

INTRODUCTION

One cannot read the story of Jeremiah without realizing life was not a bouquet of roses for this prophet of God.

From his call in 626 B.C. to the fall of Jerusalem in 586 B.C., he had one tragic circumstance after another.

Jeremiah's task was to call people to repentance.

As he did what God called him to do, his friends left him, and his enemies antagonized him.

Our text for today describes a time in Jeremiah's life when he wanted to quit.

He wanted to abandon his God-given task and settle for a life in seclusion.

If we would paraphrase Jeremiah 9:2, we would hear Jeremiah cry, "I wish I had a cabin in the woods and could get away from these people."

Have you ever felt like Jeremiah? I have been discouraged like Jeremiah and have said, "I just

feel like quitting and going to the mountains of Colorado." Discouragement faces us almost every day as we carry out the Lord's work. I am sure you have, as a Sunday School teacher, have worked as hard as you could and felt like quitting. I'm sure you as a committee member, have worked as hard as you could and felt like quitting.

I am sure you tried to be a Christian and do right, but everything goes wrong and you felt like quitting.

Why, then, should we keep going? Why don't we just quit? Why?

1. Because of the call within.

We can't quit because of the call within of God.

Jeremiah had a call from God. Listen to Jeremiah 1:4-5, "Then the word of the LORD came unto me, saying, Before I formed thee in the belly I knew thee; and before thou camest forth out of the womb I sanctified thee, and I ordained thee a prophet unto the nations."

Although Jeremiah felt inadequate to the call, although he was unsuccessful at time, although the people remained indifferent and no one seemed to care, Jeremiah could not settle for a cabin in the woods, a resting place, because he had the challenge of God burning within his heart, and he could not escape it.

Listen to his own words as Jeremiah tried to quit serving God and rest awhile. Jeremiah 20:9, "Then I said, I will not make mention of him, nor speak any more in his name. But his word was in mine heart as a burning fire shut up in my bones, and I was weary with forbearing, and I could not stay."

If you are a Christian and you try to quit serving God, you can't.

That call of God will come. "Go ye into all the world and preach the gospel to every creature."

A gray-haired Sunday School teacher became ill after many years of faithful teaching. The doctor told him he had cancer. He had only a short time to live. When the pastor visited him, the old teacher said, "Pastor, do you know what I'd like to do more than anything else in the world? I'd like to go back and teach my men's Bible class just one more time. I want to tell them that not only is Jesus a wonderful savior to live by, but He is also a wonderful savior to die by."

Our call as Christians is to serve God.

Regardless of how people respond, regardless of their hostility, regardless of their lack of understanding, we cannot quit and settle for a resting place, because the call is burning in our hearts.

2.   Because of the call without.

We cannot quit and rest from service as a Christian, not only because of an inner call but also because of a call from without.

How vivid this appeared to Jeremiah as he looked at those around him. His heart was burdened by their spiritual condition.

The people had turned from God. They were wasting their lives. They were on a self-destructing course.

Jeremiah could not give up even if he wanted to, because he was compelled by the call of help from those around him. The need and call of help is just as clear and loud as in Jeremiah's day.

When a teacher asked one of her students the shape of the world, one little girl responded, "My daddy says that it is in the worst shape it has ever been in."

The little girl was right.

Never have there been more broken homes, more ruined lives, more subtle temptations, more manifestations of sin.

Never has a generation of people had a greater need for God than ours.

Before you quit your class, before you resign from that committee, before you quit coming to visitation, before you start retiring as a Christian, as yourself this question: "If we don't do something about this need, who will?"

Jesus described the compelling impetus of this need in the story of the shepherd and the sheep in Luke 15.

At evening when the shepherd counted his sheep, 99 were safe in the pen. That's a pretty good percentage. 99% is not bad.

However, the shepherd was not concerned about percentages. He was concerned about the lost sheep.

So, he went out immediately and searched diligently for the one lost sheep.

The he laid it on his shoulders and called his friends to rejoice with him for this one lost sheep that had been found.

Even if there is only one sheep lost, only one person in need, only one individual hurting, only one Christian straying, we still must keep going.

The need without calls us out of our discouragement.

CONCLUSION

We have the answer: JESUS!

Sermon 4

We Need Men
Jeremiah 5:1

INTRODUCTION

Senator Frank Carlson of Kansas, who spent eighteen years in the U.S. Senate, made a talk at a breakfast prayer meeting on the subject, "Wanted, A Man – A Man Who Will Stand." Senator Carlson described the kind of men the world is looking for today.

The world is looking for:

Men who are not for sale;

Men who are honest, sound from center to circumference, true to the hearts core;

Men with consciences as steady as the needle to the pole;

Men who will stand for the right of the heavens and the earth reels;

Men who can tell the truth and look the world right in the eye;

Men who neither flag nor flinch;

Men who have courage without showing it;

Men in whom the courage of everlasting life runs still, deep
and strong;
Men who know their message and tell it;
Men who know their place and fill it;
Men who know their business and attend to it;
Men who will not lie, shirk, or dodge;
Men who are not too lazy to work, nor too proud to be
poor;
Men who are willing to eat what they have earned and
wear what they have paid for;
God is looking for men.

This was the cry of Jeremiah in our text. His nation was
bankrupt for the lack of men. The more Jeremiah searched
for men, the more he found they had rebelled against him.

In chapter 2, Jeremiah vividly described two arresting
characteristics of sin. First, he observed that sin is unnatural.
When a man sins, he is not behaving as God created him. Sin
is contrary to the original purpose of God. God did not so
make men to sin. Sin is a cancer upon the soul that only the
Great Physician can cut out.

Secondly, Jeremiah declared that sin is illogical. Not only
is iniquity against our original nature; indeed, it makes no
sense at all. Sin contradicts every sensible thought of man. In
other realms man uses his reason, but in sin he abandons it.

If sin is both unnatural and illogical, why do we become
involved in it? Jeremiah suggests three motives:

1. Men turn to sin in rebellion against restraint. They
    consider the laws of God too demanding, to stringent.
2. The desire to satisfy sinful lusts is a second reason men
    sin.
3. A third motive for sin is the love of money. There is
    no crime that men will not commit to get the money

they think they need. This has become all too clear in our country. In Jeremiah's day, the poor were being sacrificed upon the altar of the rich.

The consequences of sin is that it blinds men of their condition. As a result of sin in Jerusalem, the men became blinded and were no longer men. As the result of lack of real men, injustice, impurity, and oppression had resulted. There was a rebellion and contempt for God. What a sad condition for a country to get in.

That was Jerusalem hundreds of years ago. But I know a country that is in just as sad a state. Her name is the United States of America. She lacks men, real men. We live in a country like Jeremiah's, where the men have become blinded to the ways of God.

Do you know who God is going to hold responsible for the sins of this country? The children, no, the women, no, the men. Yes, children sin and women sin and they must answer for their individual sins, but the sins of this country is the result of the men not being men.

Do you know why corruption exists in our governments? Because men have become blinded to truth.

Do you know why such ungodly and inhuman acts as the slaughter of the Rockford children and others occur over and over? Because men are blinded to truth.

Jeremiah cried, "Run ye to and fro through the streets of Jerusalem and see if ye can find a man..." It just doesn't seem like men want to be men today. Why, that bunch of females that gathered in Houston ought never to have taken place and wouldn't have, if men were men. The reason the family is under such an attack today in our society is because men are not being men.

It saddens me, it hurts me, to admit the real leaders of most of our churches today are women. Oh, there are a few men, and thank God for them. But in most churches, it is the women who lead out.

Oh, how we need men!

But what kind of men do we need? Jeremiah tells us.

Men who execute judgement and men of truth.

We need men who will execute judgement.

A man who will say no to what is wrong and yes to what is right.

A lot of our troubles today is the men are not calling sin, sin.

Parents are telling their children, set their own standards today.

Instead of the parent telling the child what to do, the child tells the parents what he's going to do.

A lot of people run down the young people, they do this and that. I admit young people today are committing crimes and never being punished. A few years back they would have been hung.

It used to be when a youth started sowing his wild oats that his father started the thrashing machine. Today, the fathers have forgotten what a thrashing machine is. Men need to execute judgement. Seems men do not want to get involved anymore.

Apathy is destroying our nation, our homes, and our churches. We need men today who will get involved. Sure, it costs something to get involved and there are risks.

A few weeks back, ZI went down to the station to get a coke. One the way back, I noticed two young boys fighting on the square. I had to decide to stop the fight or pass on. I stopped and told them to break it up. Sure, they got mad at me, cussed me and one threw a beer bottle and broke it in front of me. Then they used real good judgment and jumped in their pickup and left, because by then, I was really ready to get involved.

We need men who will stand up for what's right and not be ashamed.

We need men who are seeking truth. Men who will stand up for their convictions. The trouble is that today, most men don't have faith in anything.

A cute young miss wanted her boyfriend to be a hero. So, after he was drafted, he volunteered for the parachute outfit. The instructor told him on the first jump to pull the cord with his left hand after he jumped, but if it didn't open, then pull the cord with his right hand. As they left for the jump, the instructor told them there would be a truck to pick them up and bring them back.

Then came the jump. The fellow jumped and pulled the cord with his left hand, but it didn't open. He pulled the other cord with his right hand, but it still didn't open. On the way down he was heard to say, "Nothing works in this army, so far—and I'll bet the truck won't be there to pick me up, either."

Resources

I read and gleaned insight in my study of Jeremiah from the following resources. If I quoted any resource, I noted it at the time of writing.

Dearman, J. Andrew, *The NIV Application Commentary Jeremiah, Lamentations.* Grand Rapids: Zondervan. 2002

Hearson, N. Blake and Karen Dockrey. *Jeremiah: Faithful to the Mission.* Nashville: Lifeway Press, 2019.

Huey, F. B., Jr., *The New American Commentary: Jeremiah, Lamentations,* Vol. 16. Nashville: Broadman Press, 1993.

Matthews, Lebron and Karen Dockrey, Jeremiah Faithful to the Mission Leader Guide. Nashville: Lifeway Press, 2019.

McGee, J. Vernon. *Thru the Bible Commentary Series, The Prophets Jeremiah and Lamentations.* Nashville: Thomas Nelson, 1999.

Morgan, G. Campbell. Studies in the Prophecy of Jeremiah. Grand Rapids: Fleming H. Revell 4th Printing, 1994.

Phillips, John. *Exploring the Old Testament Book by Book.* Grand Rapids: Kregel Publications, 2009.

Ryken, Phillip Graham. R. Kent Hughes Series Editor. *Preaching the Word: Jeremiah and Lamentations.* Wheaton, Illinois: Crossway, 2001.

Vines, Jerry. *Sermons on Jeremiah.* Jerry Vine Ministries, 2005.

Wiersbe, Warren W. *Be Decisive: Jeremiah.* Colorado Springs: David C. Cook, 1991.

Wood, Fred M. and Ross McLaren, General Editor Max Anders. *Holman Old Testament Commentary: Jeremiah Lamentations.* Nashville: B&H Publishing Group, 2006.

About the Author

Dr. Mike Smith,
President, Jacksonville College in Jacksonville, Texas

Dr. Smith holds several academic degrees, including an Associate of Arts from Blinn College, a Bachelor of Arts from Baylor University, and a Master of Divinity and a Master of Religious Education from Southwestern Baptist Theological Seminary in Fort Worth. He has an earned doctorate from Luther Rice Seminary, as well as a Doctor of Ministry degree and a Doctor of Philosophy degree from Southern Seminary in Louisville, Kentucky.

Dr. Smith has taught courses as Adjunct Professor at the Baptist Missionary Association Theological Seminary in Jacksonville, and for Southwestern Baptist Theological Seminary in Fort Worth. He has served on the Jacksonville College Board of Visitors, and has also been a member of the Board of Trustees for the college.

Dr. Smith pastored churches for 17 years in Texas at Gatesville, Frost, Valley View, Edom, and Terrell. He has worked with the Home Mission Board of the Southern Baptist Convention as a church planter in Illinois, and has served as 2nd Vice Chairman of the International Mission Board for the SBC. From 1995 to 2008, Smith was Director of Missions of the Dogwood Trails Baptist Area in Jacksonville. Prior to that, he was Director of Missions at Double Mountain Baptist Area in Stamford, Texas for eight years. He served as Director of the Minister/Church Relations Department for the Southern Baptists of Texas Convention for three years before becoming president of Jacksonville College in 2011. He also teaches Old and New Testament Survey courses at Jacksonville College. He starts each class day with a devotional from Proverbs and prayer.

Mike Smith has been married to Susan Springer Smith for forty-two years. They have two children, Martha Elain Gardner and Lance Curtis Smith. They have five grandchildren, William, Emma, and Jacob Gardner, and Logan and Landon Smith. they also count as their children son-in-law, James Gardner and daughter-in-law, Ashley Smith.

His other books include:

- Conflict: Causes and Cures.

- A Proverb A Day: Daily Wisdom For Living (available in English and Spanish)

- *The 5 W's of Every Old Testament Book*

- *Daily Beside The Still Waters: Devotions From Psalms*

- *31 Days of Vanity: Devotions from Ecclesiastes*

Leave A Well

Someone said, "When you go through the valley, leave a well." In other words, as we travel through this life and find a source of blessing or strength, we should do our best to help those who come behind us. We ought to leave a source of blessing for those travelers who will come behind us.

If this volume has been a blessing to you, please consider taking a few moments to leave a "Review" at site where you purchased this book. Leaving a review of at least 25 words will help others find this book and its message of hope or encouragement for them.

You can follow this link to leave a review for *Jeremiah: Unusual Sermons* on Amazon.

St. Catherine's Well, Glenwood Mission Inn,
Riverside, CA., Courtesy NYPL, Circa 1918

FRANKLIN PUBLISHING

The goal of Franklin Publishing is to enable Pastors, Evangelists, Missionaries, and Christian leaders and presenters to become published authors. Becoming a published author expands your influence and builds your ministry. You can write the book or sermon series which God has laid on your heart. We can walk that road with you.

www.FranklinPublishing.org

Come and visit our Facebook page and be sure to like and follow us to keep up with writing tips and new developments.

www.facebook.com/FranklinPublishing

A Word of Hope from Jeremiah

11 For I know the plans I have for you," declares the LORD, "plans to prosper you and not to harm you, plans to give you hope and a future.

Jeremiah 29:11 (NIV)

Made in the USA
Columbia, SC
27 June 2021